Just Play It... with Attitude!

Six Early Intermediate Level
Piano Solos
by
Carolyn Miller

Contents

12135E

Rockin'

Allegro moderato

Carolyn Miller

L.H.
R.H.
R.H.
L.H.

Movin'

Allegro moderato ♩ = 137

Carolyn Miller

R.H.
L.H.

Steppin' Out

Allegro moderato

Carolyn Miller

f
L.H.
R.H.

Spanish Holiday

Moderato ♩ = 125

Carolyn Miller

mp
mf
mp
f

Swingin'

Allegro moderato

Carolyn Miller

mf

f
mf

Jazz-a-ma-tazz

Moderato

Carolyn Miller

f
mf
R.H.
1 2 4 3
5
R.H.
2 3
f L.H.
R.H.
1 4

mf
R.H.
R.H.
R.H.
f L.H.